TENNIS

Keith Reynolds

RIGBY

INTERACTIVE
LIBRARY

© 1997 Reed Educational & Professional Publishing
Published by Rigby Interactive Library,
an imprint of Reed Educational & Professional Publishing,
500 Coventry Lane,
Crystal Lake, IL 60014

Produced by Mandarin Offset Ltd., Hong Kong
Printed in China
Designed by Ron Kamen, Green Door Design
Illustrated by Barry Atkinson

02 01 00 99 98
10 9 8 7 6 5 4 3 2 1

Reynolds, Keith, 1947-
   Tennis / Keith Reynolds.
      p.   cm. – (Successful sports)
   Includes bibliographical references and index.
   Summary: Briefly describes the equipment, skills, tactics, and rules involved in tennis.
   ISBN 1-57572-200-3 (lib. bdg.)
   1. Tennis – Juvenile literature. [1. Tennis.] I. Title. II. Series.
GV996.5.R493 1997
796.342 – dc21   96-52604
                                                    CIP
                                                      AC

Acknowledgments
The publisher would like to thank the following for permission to reproduce photographs: Action Plus: p. 22; Allsport: pp. 7, 13, 15, 19, 27, 28, 29; Colorsport: title page and pp. 8, 11, 26; Sporting Pictures: pp. 10, 24; Mike Liles: pp. 6, 21; Meg Sullivan: pp. 4, 9, 14, 17, 20, 23, 25. Cover photograph © Allsport.

The cover photo shows Mary Jo Fernandez in action at Wimbledon. The title page shows Gabrielle Sabatini.

The publishers and author would like to thank the Watchorn Tennis Club, Steve Buchanan, and Keeth Elementary School for their help with the photographs.

Note to the Reader
Some words in this book are printed in bold type. This indicates that the word is listed in the glossary on page 30. The glossary gives a brief explanation of words that may be new to you.

Contents

The Court and Equipment

The modern game of tennis, officially known as "lawn tennis," is a game for two or four people, played on a special court. The players use their tennis rackets to hit the ball back and forth to each other over a net. Today, tennis is played throughout the world and is a popular sport for competition, exercise, and fun. Players of all ages can enjoy tennis, but it is easiest to learn when young.

Tennis can be played on many kinds of surfaces, such as grass, clay, cement, wood, asphalt, and **synthetic** materials. The chief requirement is that the ball bounces the same way every time it hits the court without being too slow or too fast. Normally, tennis courts are open-air, and in suitable climates the game is played outdoors. Many countries also have indoor courts so that tennis can be played all year round.

Good tennis clothes not only help you play better, but are also comfortable and attractive.

An official tennis court is a flat, rectangular playing area with double-side boundary lines 78 feet long. An outer set of lines down the sides of the court marks a width of $31\frac{1}{2}$ feet and an inner set marks a width of 27 feet. There needs to be plenty of flat space on the sides and back of the marked court. This area is known as the run-back area. The court is divided into two halves by a net that is 3 feet high and brushes the ground.

The net is usually made of nylon. When two people are playing tennis against each other, in a game known as **singles**, the inner set of sidelines form the boundary of the court.

If four people are playing in a **doubles** match, then the outer lines are the side boundaries and a longer net is used to cover the full width of the court.

Pointers

Try not to play with a racket that is too big or heavy. A light, comfortable racket enables you to control the ball better.

Tennis clothes should be comfortable and allow you to run around easily. Male players usually wear shorts and open-necked, short-sleeved shirts. Female players use similar clothing but can also wear short skirts instead of shorts, or one-piece tennis dresses. Good shoes are very important for traction on the court and to support the feet. Outdoors in cold weather you may want to wear a sweatsuit when practicing or playing.

The most important piece of equipment used by a tennis player is the racket. In the past, the frame of a tennis racket was made of wood. Today, special materials, such as graphite and aluminium, make the rackets lighter and more powerful. But these new materials also make rackets more expensive. The racket strings are usually made out of synthetic materials that are waterproof and long-lasting.

Tennis courts cover large areas. You have to be very fit to play singles well.

Tennis balls are hollow rubber covered with a type of felt made of dacron, nylon, and wool. It is important to play with quality tennis balls because they make the game easier. A ball clip is a useful item. This small plastic cup fits onto your waistband and holds the second ball when you are serving.

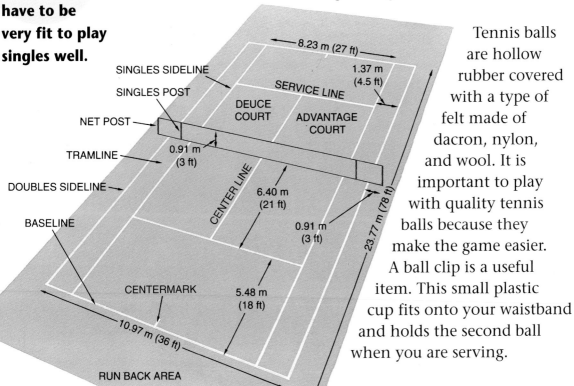

SINGLES SIDELINE
SINGLES POST
NET POST
TRAMLINE
DOUBLES SIDELINE
BASELINE
CENTERMARK
RUN BACK AREA

8.23 m (27 ft)
1.37 m (4.5 ft)
SERVICE LINE
DEUCE COURT
ADVANTAGE COURT
0.91 m (3 ft)
CENTER LINE
6.40 m (21 ft)
0.91 m (3 ft)
23.77 m (78 ft)
5.48 m (18 ft)
10.97 m (36 ft)

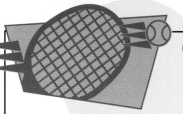

The Fundamentals

Watching the ball

In tennis, the type of shot a player chooses depends on where and how fast the **opponent** has hit the ball. To make sure they choose the correct shot, good players must keep their eyes on the ball all the time it is in the air and watch to see how it bounces. To make sure the ball goes where they want, they watch it even more carefully as they hit it. The ball then successfully travels back over the net to the opponent and the whole process begins again. This back-and-forth returning of the ball is called **rallying**.

Moving to the ball

Good tennis players can move very quickly. They watch the ball and learn to judge where and how it will land. This gives them time to get to it. This also means that they will have better ball control. They always make sure they get balanced before they hit the ball back.

This girl is watching closely as she hits a forehand.

Good players remember that their opponents will try to run to the shot they have just hit. If they stand still after they have played their shot, they make it easier for their opponent. So they always run back to the middle of the **baseline** as soon as they can.

The stroke

In a tennis match players have to use different types of racket movement to hit the ball how and where they want to. These movements are known as "strokes."

Pointers

Try to use different grips for the forehands and backhands. Most juniors find it easier to play a backhand using two hands (a *double-handed grip*), but hold the racket with only one hand for the forehand.

Top players like American Michael Chang do a lot of stretching exercises so they can return difficult shots, like this one at the French Open.

A tennis game is scored by points. All points begin with a **serve**. In this stroke, the server throws the ball above the racket and hits it to the other side of the net before it touches the ground. A powerful serve can be difficult for the opponent to return.

For right-handed players, shots played on the right side of the body are called **forehands** and those on the left **backhands**. For left-handed players, it is the other way around.

If a player is close to the net and hits the ball before it bounces, the stroke is called a **volley**. If the ball is hit after it bounces, it is called a **groundstroke**. The volley is a short, forward, punching-type movement, but a groundstroke is a true swing.

Another way of hitting the ball is with the **smash**. In this stroke a player stands near the net and reaches high for the ball, hitting it sharply from above the head.

A **lob** is a high shot that arcs through the air toward the back of the court. A lob is useful because it forces the opponent to move back away from the net.

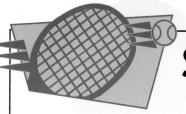

Serving

Since a player has the best chance to score points when serving, having a good serve is very important. It is the only time when a player has a chance to hit the ball without it first having come over the net from the opponent. This means it can be practiced alone. The very best players in the world generally have excellent serves that are so fast and so accurate that their opponents have no chance to return the ball. Such serves are called **aces**.

Because a server can choose to aim anywhere into the service box (see court diagram, p. 5) and is allowed two attempts, good players always try to serve to their opponent's worst stroke. Then their opponent is forced to use a weak **return of serve**.

If the serve does not go over the net and into the service box, it is called a **fault**. If this happens on the second chance, it is a **double fault** and the opponent wins the point. So, the second serve has to be a carefully performed, safe shot to prevent this from happening.

To develop the best possible serve, it is important that the different parts of the body work together. Timing must be perfect.

During Wimbledon 1994, Boris Becker of Germany shows how you can hit the ball very hard with a good service action.

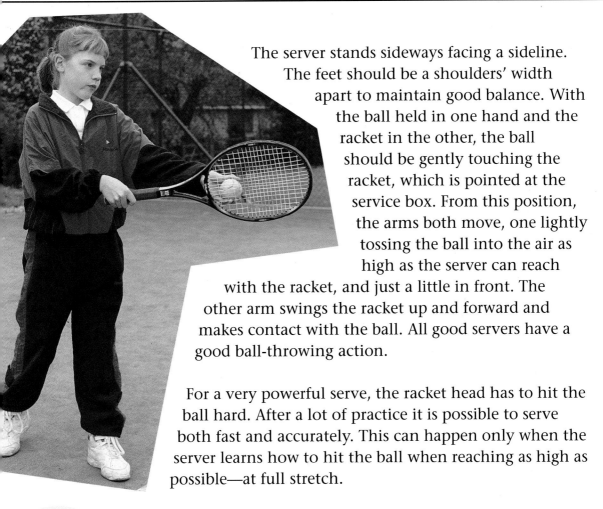

The server stands sideways facing a sideline. The feet should be a shoulders' width apart to maintain good balance. With the ball held in one hand and the racket in the other, the ball should be gently touching the racket, which is pointed at the service box. From this position, the arms both move, one lightly tossing the ball into the air as high as the server can reach with the racket, and just a little in front. The other arm swings the racket up and forward and makes contact with the ball. All good servers have a good ball-throwing action.

For a very powerful serve, the racket head has to hit the ball hard. After a lot of practice it is possible to serve both fast and accurately. This can happen only when the server learns how to hit the ball when reaching as high as possible—at full stretch.

This player shows the proper set-up before serving. Her body is facing a sideline, the ball is lightly touching the racket, and she is concentrating on where she wants to serve the ball.

In serving, the best way to hold the racket is with the **chopper grip** because this helps the player to hit the ball hard and fast (or **flat**). By turning the wrist a little bit, the ball can be made to **spin**. This helps the server get the ball to an exact point in the service box, making it difficult for the opponent to return.

TENNIS FACTS

In order to control how fast serves can be hit, tennis authorities have experimented with different tennis balls at the major tournaments. At Wimbledon they used slow balls. But at the French Open, on their long rally clay courts, they used fast balls.

Returning

Top tennis players practice their return of serve shots as much as they practice their serves. This is because they expect their opponents to have very good serves that are hard to return. The serve can be returned only after the ball has bounced. This makes a service return very similar to other forehand and backhand groundstrokes. Because the server can aim to bounce the ball anywhere in the service box and can hit the ball as fast or slow as he or she likes, the returner has to be ready to play any one of a selection of different shots.

If the serve is hit very hard, the returner just tries to get the ball back over the net. But if the service is very slow, the returner has the opportunity to play an **attacking shot**. The first serve is often the best. If the server miss-hits it, and it lands in the net or out-of-bounds, then he or she has one more chance to get a **second serve** in. When the second attempt also fails to be a **legal** serve, then the returner gets the point without ever touching the ball. A good server can aim the serve to an opponent's forehand or backhand, so it is important for players to master both shots.

A wide stance and a low, ready-to-spring position are important for good returns, as German Steffi Graf shows during the 1994 Australian Open.

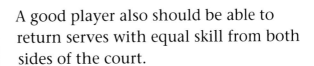

A good player also should be able to return serves with equal skill from both sides of the court.

Because the server may be able to hit the serve very fast into the corners of the box, the returner must be well-prepared by adopting the correct **stance**. A good stance is facing the server, with the feet just wider apart than the width of the shoulders. The racket face should be pointing at the server and the returner should be ready to move either to the right or the left.

If the server has a fast and accurate serve, the returner can start by standing just behind the baseline. If the server misses the first serve, or has a weak serve, the returner can move forwards a little and get ready to attack. Standing behind the service box in the right place is vital for the best chance of a good return.

Look at the diagram on page 18 and you will see that the returner must concentrate on three important things:
First: Where is the server standing?
Second: Where is the middle of the service box?
Third: How far back should I be standing?

A good serve can dominate the match. American Pete Sampras shows how during the 1994 Wimbledon men's final.

When the returner is in the correct **ready position**, it is now time to look at the ball. Good returners watch the ball all the time, even when it is in the server's hand. They follow it as the server throws it up, and when he or she hits it they keep looking at the ball all the time it is traveling toward them. In this way good returners can **anticipate** when and where the ball will bounce and make sure they move quickly to the best returning position. The returner's eyes stay on the ball at all times especially when hitting the return shot to place it exactly where they want in the server's side of the court.

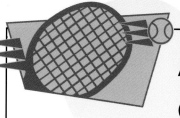

At the Back of the Court

One of the most important places players learn to aim for is deep into the back corners of the opponent's court. Hitting shots to one back corner and then the other will force the other player to run from side to side, and will stop them from attacking. If one opponent hits the ball slow and short, the other tries to hit the ball even harder and farther. This is how tennis players hit **winners**. Even if a player is good and can run to all the opponent's best shots, the opponent can still win by not missing the return shots and keeping the ball in play. This is called being **consistent**. The average length of a rally is only four or five shots, so being consistent can make a player much harder to beat.

Groundshots are easier to hit when the ball is falling and contact is at a comfortable height.

It is very important for a player to have enough control to hit the ball over the net at different heights for different shots. Hard-hit groundstrokes have to be kept lower than slow shots. Otherwise a player might overhit and the ball might go out of bounds. Defensive shots need to be higher, so that they land deep and give the hitter time to recover.

A player also needs to run for every ball to be able to beat the opponent. Some beginners make the mistake of running to a ball, hitting it, and then stopping to look where it has gone before moving back to a good ready position.

The best players always get back quickly to the center of the baseline as soon as they have finished their stroke, so that they are waiting for their opponent's next shot.

The way a player successfully hits a groundstroke to the desired spot in the opponent's court is by knowing when to make contact with it. A good player does not hit the ball immediately after it bounces, but waits until it begins to fall again. Most successful forehand shots are hit when the ball is about hip high.

In order to make sure they hit the ball at the most comfortable height and distance, good players are always ready to run forward, backward, and sideways. The ball bounces very differently depending on the opponent's shot.

Once a player has learned how to watch the ball, he or she can prepare for the groundstroke by taking the racket back even before the ball has bounced. This movement should be smooth and controlled. If a player can control the racket, then the racket will be able to control the ball.

Learning to hit a double-handed backhand is a big advantage for beginners. Arantxa Sanchez-Vicario of Spain demonstrates one at the U.S. Open.

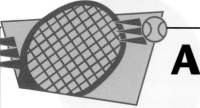

At the Net

Some of the shots an opponent hits are not hit very hard, so they must be played from near the net. The strokes most likely to be used from very close to the net are volleys and smashes. These shots are hit before the ball has bounced. When a returner plays a shot from close to the net, he or she often tries to hit the ball as far away from the opponent as possible. This is called an **angled shot**.

A player needs to be very alert and quick when coming to the net because volleys and smashes do not give not much time to react. Having a good ready position is therefore very important.

Confident players often play close to the net. Playing near the net gives a player the chance to hit winning volleys and smashes. Also, the opponent will find it very difficult to hit the ball low into the back of the player's court.

Hitting smashes can help you win other points, because you feel so confident.

Pointers

In the quick volleys near the net, it is very important to keep your wrist firm to keep your racket head steady. Grip the racket quite firmly and squeeze it even tighter, just as the ball hits, for extra control.

When players are close to the net and are volleying, they don't swing the racket. With so little time before the racket meets the ball, they usually use a short, punching action. This is true for both backhand and forehand volleys. Many top players' favorite shot to play from close to the net is a fast and powerful overhead smash. All of the player's strength goes into the shot, which is similar in technique to the serve.

In volleying, the best grip to use is the chopper, because the play can be very fast and there is often not enough time to shift the hand position between shots. Both forehand and backhand volleys, as well as smashes, can be hit with this same grip.

Sweden's Stefan Edberg and other top players often use serving and volleying because it helps them take charge of the rally.

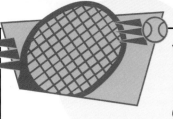

Your Opponent at the Net

Defending the net involves choosing shots that make it difficult for an opponent to get up close and hit winners. The two best shots to use when an opponent has managed to get up to the net are the lob and the **passing shot**.

When a player lobs the ball high over the net, the ball should land as far behind the opponent as possible. A passing shot also tries to get the ball behind the opponent, but this time by going down on one side of him or her. In both cases, it is not possible for the other player to reach the ball without moving for it. If the opponent has to run for the ball, then it is unlikely that he or she will be able to play a controlled shot.

Another way a player can beat an opponent who is near the net is to hit the ball low over the net into the front of the court. The opponent cannot return this low shot too hard because it will have to be hit upwards to get it over the net. The other player will then have a slow, easy shot to lob or hit as a passing shot.

With lobs and passing shots, good players are able to judge very carefully a good time to "wrong-foot" their opponents.

Pointers

Topspin can be very useful on passing shots. It makes the ball dip toward the ground so the opponent doesn't have the chance to hit an easy high volley.

When the opponent is at the net, good players get in as difficult a shot as possible.

Forehand

Backhand

Serve

This usually forces them to make a mistake. Lobs are more difficult to return if they are aimed at the opponent's backhand. Also, it makes it much more difficult for the other player to return a lob when facing the sun, or hitting into the wind. With passing shots, good players can position the ball just where they want it to land in their opponent's court. If they hit it too close to the other player, then that sets up an easy volley. If it's too wide of their opponent, the point may be lost if it goes out of the court.

If a player doesn't hit ground shots deep enough, the opponent can run up close in to the net after hitting the ball. This is called playing an **approach shot**. When an opponent plays a good approach shot, a player may be forced into lobbing the ball. If the approach shot is weaker, the player may be able to try a passing shot. The goal is to try to keep the opponent as far from the net as possible. This gives a player the choice of either going to the net, or beating the opponent from the back of the court.

Having the correct grips for forehand, backhand and serve is very important because they make it easier to control the racket head.

Doubles

The tennis game of doubles is played by four people, two on each side. Since doubles is a fast, attacking type of tennis, it is good **tactics** for both players to try to get close to the net. A team then has a much better chance of hitting winners and finding an undefended space to hit into between the opponents. Sometimes they will find it difficult to decide who should go for a ball that lands between them.

Players with good volleys and smashes are often very good doubles players. This is because they can stand near the net in a perfect attacking position while their **partner** is either serving or returning from the baseline. In the best doubles teams, both players are always alert and watching the ball even if their partners are serving or returning. Both players need to use the same **strategy** to make a winning team.

Pointers

In doubles, if your opponents make a weak return, the player nearest the net has a chance to hit your opponents' shot before it goes deeper in the court. This is called an "interception" and can often lead to your team winning the point.

Make sure you are standing in the correct position before the point begins.

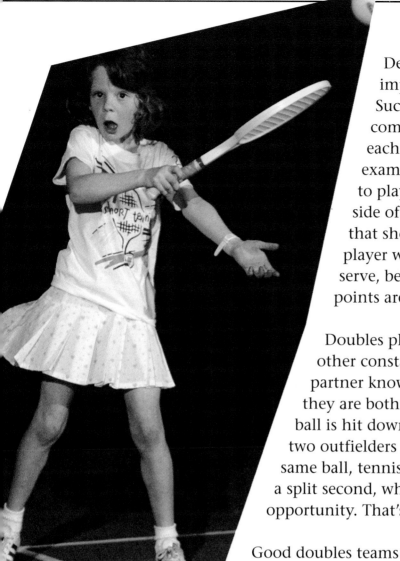

Developing strategy is important in doubles. Successful doubles teams combine the strengths of each individual player. For example, choosing which side to play: the backhand, or left side of the court, is the position that should be played by the player with the best return of serve, because many critical points are served to that side.

Doubles players also talk to each other constantly. They must let their partner know where they are in case they are both going for a lob, or if a ball is hit down the middle. Just like two outfielders in baseball going for the same ball, tennis players must decide, in a split second, who has the better shot opportunity. That's teamwork!

Good doubles teams practice together. When they are practicing, they try to recreate match situations, such as net play, groundstrokes from the baseline, and switching sides during a point. This way partners learn how to support each other and how best to win the match.

A good return is the best way to start a point. A strong return can allow partners to get to the net and be aggressive.

Pointers

The best way to avoid injury when you start playing tennis is to use the correct equipment, including properly fitted shoes. Also, always warm up your muscles and joints by doing some exercises before practicing or playing a match.

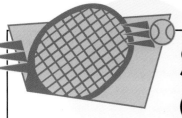

Scoring and Other Rules

Scoring a match

A tennis match is scored using a system of points, games, and sets. To score a point, a player or doubles team has to hit a shot the other player or team does not return. The points are added up, and when a player or team has scored four points, and is at least two points ahead of the other side, then the game is won.

Because you get two chances with a serve, using a ball clip for the second ball leaves both hands free to help control the racket when the rally begins.

The points in tennis all have individual names. The first point scored is called 15, the second is called 30, the third is called 40, and the fourth is known as the **game point**. If you have no points, then your score is said to be **love**. Another name is used when both sides have three points each. Instead of being called 40–40, it is known as **deuce**. When the score reaches deuce, one side has to win two more points to win the game. If one side gains one more point, then that side has the **advantage point**. If it goes back to a tie score then it is called deuce again. Only after winning two points in a row from deuce can a side win game point and take the game.

The first side to reach six games wins the set. When there are equal game scores of 6–6, a **tiebreaker** game is necessary. Scoring a tiebreaker game is different from scoring a normal game. The side whose turn it is to serve serves for the first point. Then each side in turn serves twice. The tiebreaker ends when one player or team has scored seven points and is at least two points ahead. The winner will have won the set by 7–6.

Tennis can be a singles or a team game. Good doubles players always try to help each other.

To win a tennis match, one player or team usually needs to win two sets. In some men's competitions, the winning players must take three sets to win a match.

Playing a game

Before starting the first game of a match, the players need to decide who will serve first. This is usually done by tossing a coin or spinning a racket. The winner of the call can decide to return or serve first, or choose which end of the court to start in. The first person serving always serves into the deuce box. After that, it alternates with every point of the game that is played. The player returning the serve has to let the ball bounce in the service court before hitting it.

When the first game is over, the players must switch ends of the court, and then it is the other player's turn to serve. End changes take place when the number of games played adds up to an odd number, for example, after game one, three, five, and so on. The match continues in this way until one player has two sets, winning each by at least two games, unless it goes to a tiebreaker.

Pointers

When there is no umpire, sometimes players forget what the score of a match is. When this happens they must start playing again from a score they can both agree upon.

When playing for fun or at school, you will probably have to do your own scoring and make sure you follow the rules of tennis. In tournaments and in all professional matches, there is an umpire. Umpires decide whether balls are out-of-bounds or if serves have landed within the service box. In games without an umpire, players are expected to call balls in or out on their own side of the court.

Junior Competitions

For young people who get involved in tennis, a wide range of junior competitions is available at all levels. They range from tournaments for eight-year-olds, to those for eighteen-year-olds involving international travel. Juniors may even play at such famous places as Wimbledon.

Tennis competitions for young people are set up through many organizations such as schools, park districts, and tennis clubs. They are usually arranged by age group.

The top junior players soon join the international circuit, but they all start by playing local competitions. Jamie Delgado is playing at Wimbledon in this photo.

Locally, many young people play at tennis clubs, and these are ideal places to start playing in real matches. Often a senior member of the club will arrange junior team matches against other nearby clubs. Sometimes several local club teams will form a league and play matches against one another.

There are also special tournaments arranged for young beginner players at local clubs. These are called Starter Competitions. Hundreds of junior tournaments are directly organized by the U.S. Tennis Association.

Players who take part are given a tennis rating number. This shows how good a tennis player is, compared to other juniors. The more matches a player wins, the better (and lower number) his or her rating becomes.

Some competitions are especially for players who have certain ratings. It helps players prepare when they know they will be playing against others of the same ability.

Once players receive ratings, they can enter tournaments, though some are open to players at any level. There are very formal programs, such as the Excellence classes for advanced players that are held mostly in major cities in the United States, or school teams that compete in leagues. Also, many tennis clubs and park districts have teams that travel throughout a particular city or a particular region. There is a tournament or league for every level. If you want to become involved, check with your local school or park district or club.

Both winning and losing can be enjoyable if you have tried your very best.

Junior tennis competitions are played in almost all countries and the juniors who want to become professional players travel to the most important international tournaments. One of these is the European Junior Tennis Championship. Another important one is the Orange Bowl Championship held in Florida every January.

TENNIS FACTS

A successful junior or professional tennis player will often get sponsored to use certain rackets, clothes or shoes. This can create a positive image for the sponsor and add to the player's income.

Famous players such as Stefan Edberg of Sweden, Steffi Graf of Germany, and Czeck-born Ivan Lendl, all won junior championships early in their careers. Even for junior players there are international ranking lists, so it is possible for one boy and one girl to say that they are the best junior players in the world.

Professional Tournaments

Any player can become a professional and accept money for playing, but only the best players generally turn professional. This is because the costs of travel, coaching, and equipment could end up being more than an inexperienced professional can earn. Male players can declare themselves to be professional players at any age, but female players have to be at least sixteen years old.

Even after deciding to turn professional, which tournaments players can take part in depends upon their world ranking position. This is the order of merit for professionals. The number is generated by a computer that collects all the results from every professional tournament in the world. An individual player's ranking is always changing because the **ranking points** awarded depend upon what players he or she has beaten, in which round of a tournament the win took place, and on the importance of the tournament.

A professional player's ranking is very important. This is because only those players with the highest rankings are invited to play in some important tournaments. Tournaments with high prize money often are the most important and carry the most ranking points. Players' ranking points are worked out annually so they keep the points they win at a tournament for one year only. When that tournament is played again the following year, new points are available to win again. This gives the new players a chance to improve their rankings compared to the more experienced professionals.

It is important to practice returning serves because the serves today are so fast—American Andre Agassi shows how!

Almost every player begins in the lowest prize money tournaments. Prize money, no matter where a tournament is played, has to be paid in American dollars. The prize money at beginner professional tournaments for men is $25,000, and for women it is $10,000. The highest total prize money in the famous international tournaments is more than $3 million, but there are many prize levels in between.

Choose the right racket for your height and strength.

Professional tournaments are arranged by a country's national tennis association and by the Association of Tennis Professionals. But a country cannot arrange a tournament whenever it likes, because it has to ask the International Tennis Federation, and in Europe also the European Tennis Federation, for permission. This is because sometimes there are tournaments arranged in other countries at the same time. The most famous professional tournaments where national teams compete are the Davis Cup for men, and the Federation Cup for women. Every tennis-playing nation tries to win these tournaments and take home the trophies.

Throughout the world professional men players have to become members of the Association of Tennis Professionals (ATP). Women professionals join the Women's Tennis Association (WTA). These associations also arrange their own tournaments.

TENNIS FACTS

At an important professional match, there are as many as twenty people on the court—one umpire, one net judge, ten linesmen, six ballboys or ballgirls, and two players.

Before every professional tournament, there is what is known as a qualifying tournament. This is where young professional players who have no ranking points can begin their tennis careers. If they win in the qualifying tournament, they are then allowed to play in the main event tournament.

Famous Places

Although tennis tournaments are played throughout the world, there are four tennis clubs that organize the most famous and important tennis events. They are the Lawn Tennis Championships, held in London; the French Open, held in Paris; the U.S. Open held in New York City; and the Australian Open, held in Melbourne. Together, they are known as the Grand Slam tournaments.

The Wimbledon Championships

There has been a tournament held in south London at Wimbledon since 1877. Many players say that it is the tournament they most want to win because it is the oldest and most famous of the open tennis tournaments.

The Wimbledon tournament is played on grass courts in the last week of June and first week of July. Wimbledon became a very profitable tournament during the 1980s. Much the profits go to the Lawn Tennis Association, to help support tennis and tennis teaching in Great Britain.

This photograph shows the outside of Center Court at Wimbledon.

The French Open

The French championships began in 1891 and have been played at Stade Roland Garros since 1921. The stadium itself is owned by the City of Paris and once the tournament has finished, anyone can play on the courts.

The French Open is played every year from the end of May to the beginning of June. The courts on which the championships are played are clay. This type of court is not as fast as a grass court. Sometimes the ball may be hit 20 to 30 times over the net before anyone can win a point.

The U.S. Open

The U.S. Open Tournament, held in early September every year, has been played in New York City at Flushing Meadows since 1978. Flushing Meadows is located very close to one of New York's most important airports. As a result, it is very noisy when planes take off and land nearby. The tennis court surface at Flushing Meadows is a type of cement called Decoturf, which has layers of rubber built into it to make it more comfortable for the players.

To be a good clay court player, you have to be very fit and patient. American Michael Chang won the French Open when he was very young.

The Australian Open

Although this tournament takes place in early January, it is regarded as the last of the Grand Slam championships for the year. The Australian Open had to move from one club to another because it grew too popular. Originally, it was played in Melbourne at Kooyong Tennis Club on grass courts. Since 1988 it has been played at Flinders Park in Melbourne, which was specially built for this tournament.

Famous Faces

I t is very difficult for players to win even one of the Grand Slam tournaments. To do it, they must win every match they play over the two-week period of top-class tennis. It is even more difficult to win all four. Very few players throughout the history of tennis have done that, especially because it requires playing on the different types of court surface.

In the last thirty years, only one man and two women have accomplished this feat. The great Australian player Rod Laver did twice, in 1962 and 1969. Margaret Smith Court, also from Australia, won all four in 1970, and Steffi Graf of Germany did the complete Grand Slam in 1988. Even the famous Swedish player Bjorn Borg, who won Wimbledon a record five times in a row, and won the French Open title six times, could never win the U.S. Open.

The youngest male winner of a Grand Slam title was Michael Chang, who was only seventeen when he won the French Open in 1989. The youngest female player to win a Grand Slam title was American player Tracy Austin. She was only sixteen when she first won the U.S. Open in 1979.

Tennis has made many men and women very famous and rich. Bjorn Borg of Sweden holds the trophy up after winning Wimbledon in 1976.

Perhaps the greatest player of modern times is Martina Navratilova. Born in Czechoslovakia in 1956, she left her native country to train and play in the United States, and finally became a U.S. citizen. During a long and successful singles and doubles career, she won the Wimbledon title nine times and the U.S. Open title four times. Navratilova retired from competitive singles tennis in 1994.

In the last twenty years, Sweden has become an important tennis center producing Bjorn Borg, Mats Wilander, and Stefan Edberg. Czechoslovakia has also produced a number of famous players, including Ivan Lendl, Martina Navratilova, Jan Kodes, and Hana Mandlikova.

But the United States continues to be the most consistent training ground for great players. The most well-known players include Chris Evert, Jimmy Connors, John McEnroe, Pete Sampras, Jim Courier and Andre Agassi. In recent years, Germany has also produced great players such as Boris Becker, Michael Stich, and Steffi Graf.

One of the most inspirational players was American Arthur Ashe, who in 1968 was the first African American to win the U.S. men's national singles championship. He turned pro in 1969 and won Wimbledon in 1975. He later coached Davis Cup teams and wrote important books about tennis.

United States tennis players have also done well in the Olympics. In 1996 in Atlanta, Andre Agassi won the men's singles, Lindsay Davenport won the women's singles, and Mary Jo and Gigi Fernandez claimed the women's doubles prize.

Mary Jo Fernandez and her partner Gigi Fernadez won consecutive gold medals in the doubles competition— in Barcelona in 1992 and Atlanta in 1996.

Glossary

ace a service that the opponent cannot return.

advantage point the next point after "deuce" and a game point to either the server or the returner.

angled shot a ball that is placed away from an opponent so that it approaches the sideline, not the baseline.

anticipate to guess from the opponent's style and court movements where the next ball will land.

approach shot the shot that enables a player to approach the net.

attacking shot any type of shot that puts the opponent under pressure. It can be a groundstroke or a volley.

backhand a groundstroke played while reaching across the body. Players who are right-handed play across their left side.

baselines the lines that mark the ends of the court.

chopper grip a special grip that allows a player to play volleys, smashes, and serves without ever having to change grip position.

consistent having the skill to perform at the same level on a regular basis. A player who is usually good at keeping the ball in play is called a consistent player. A player who cannot keep the ball going is called inconsistent.

deuce when the score in a game is 40–40.

doubles a tennis match where two pairs of players compete against each other in teams.

double-handed grip a way of holding the racket, especially for the backhand, using both hands.

fault/double fault missing a serve. A double fault gives the point to the opponent because the server missed on both serves.

flat hitting the ball without any spin.

forehand a groundstroke shot played away from the body. A right-handed player would play a forehand to the right of the body.

game point the final point needed to win a game.

groundstroke any stroke in which the ball is hit after it has bounced.

interception when the player nearest the net in a doubles match manages to move across and hit a return volley after the other team has hit a ball toward the back of the court.

legal any in-bounds shot hit according to the rules of tennis.

lob a shot hit to a position high over the head of an opponent, usually when the opponent is very near the net.

love when a player or team has no points.

opponent the person or persons a player or pair is playing against.

partner teammate in doubles matches.

passing shot a shot hit past an opponent who is at the net.

rally the back-and-forth hitting of the ball between the players.

ranking points special points given to professional players that are used to list in order the best players in the world.

ready position the position players stand in while they wait for a serve or to return a shot.

return of serve the shot played back after the service has been delivered.

second serve the serve that follows a first service fault.

serve the shot that begins every point in a tennis match. It must bounce on the correct side of the front of the court before it is returned.

singles a tennis match with one player on each side competing against each other.

slice a type of ball spin that makes the ball rotate backwards.

smash an overhead shot in which the racket is brought down at the ball, similar to a service action.

spin the motion given to a ball that makes it rotate very quickly.

sponsors individuals or businesses who give money to support tennis tournaments and tours.

stance the position in which a player stands.

strategy a specific plan used to win.

synthetic manufactured, not natural, material.

tactics the actions used to carry out a plan for winning a match. This is particularly important in doubles in which the partners need to work together.

tiebreaker the method of finalizing a set when the score reaches six games all.

topspin a type of spin that makes the ball rotate forward.

volley a shot hit before the ball has bounced.

winner any shot that an opponent cannot return.

Index